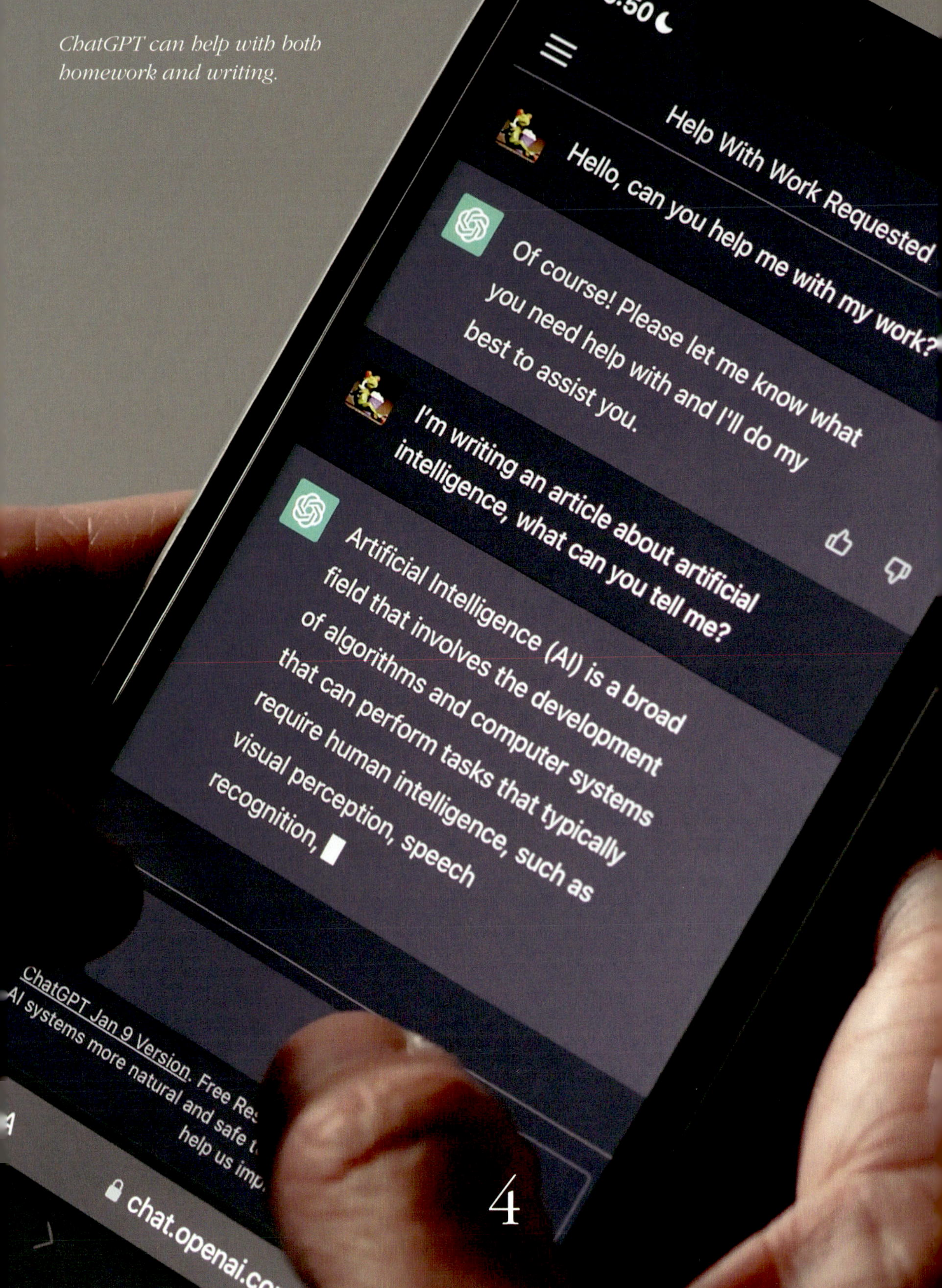

ChatGPT can help with both homework and writing.

AI IN THE WORLD

12 USES FOR ARTIFICIAL INTELLIGENCE IN EDUCATION

BLACK RABBIT BOOKS

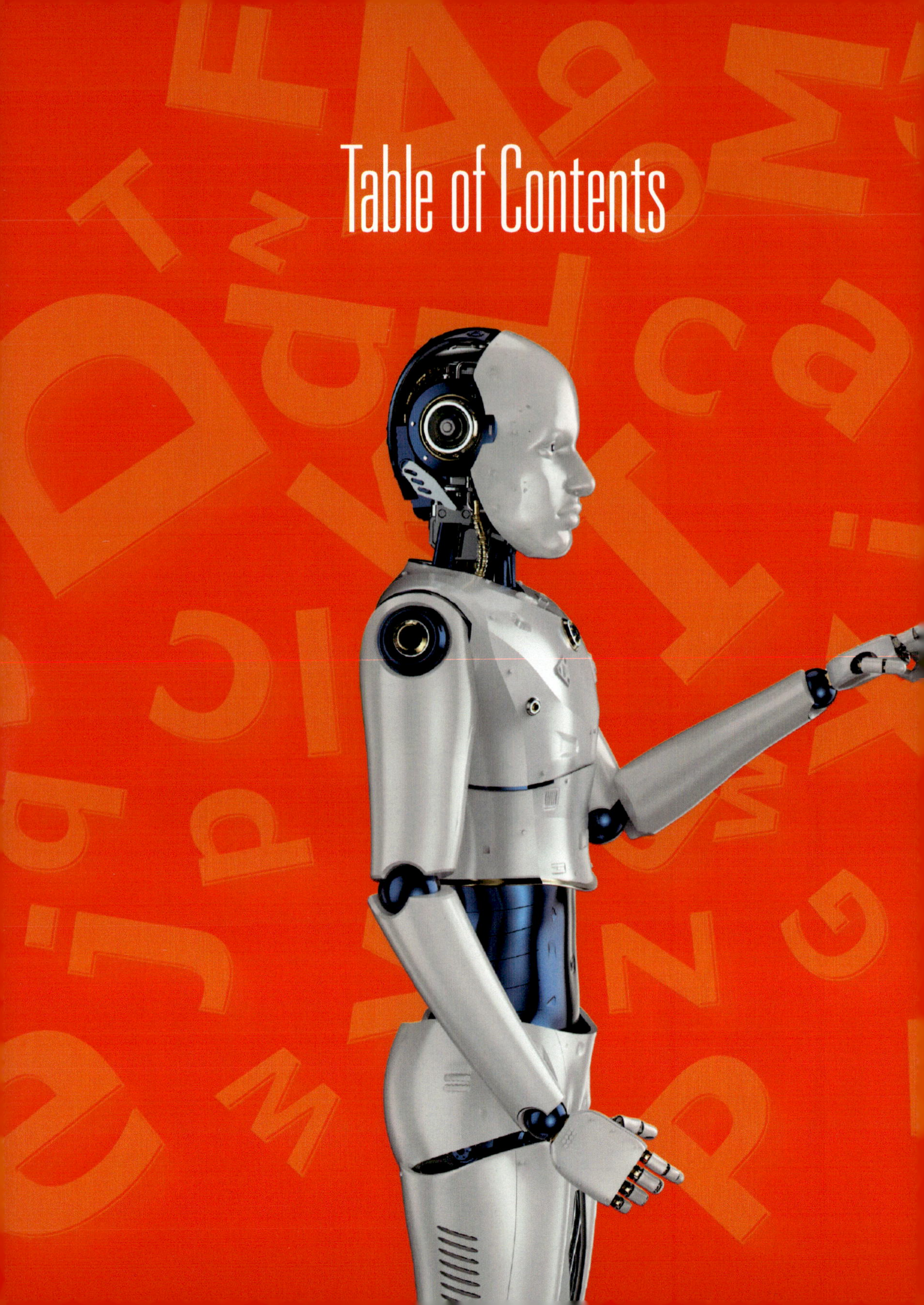

Table of Contents

AI Tools Make Learning *More Personalized*

1

Artificial Intelligence (AI) tools are computer systems that copy the way your brain works. Intelligence is the ability to learn and use what you learn. You use it to solve problems and make choices. AI can help you write, do research, and learn math skills. AI tools give **feedback**. They change the content and speed of lessons. They make choices based on your needs.

ChatGPT is a chatbot. A chatbot is a program that talks with you. First, you enter a **prompt**. "Help me learn about the solar system." Then ChatGPT scans a lot of **data**. It searches the internet. It reads online books and research papers. It reports basic facts about the solar system. It seems like a real person answered you. ChatGPT is faster than a traditional search engine. But be careful! ChatGPT may make mistakes or report false information that can seem true.

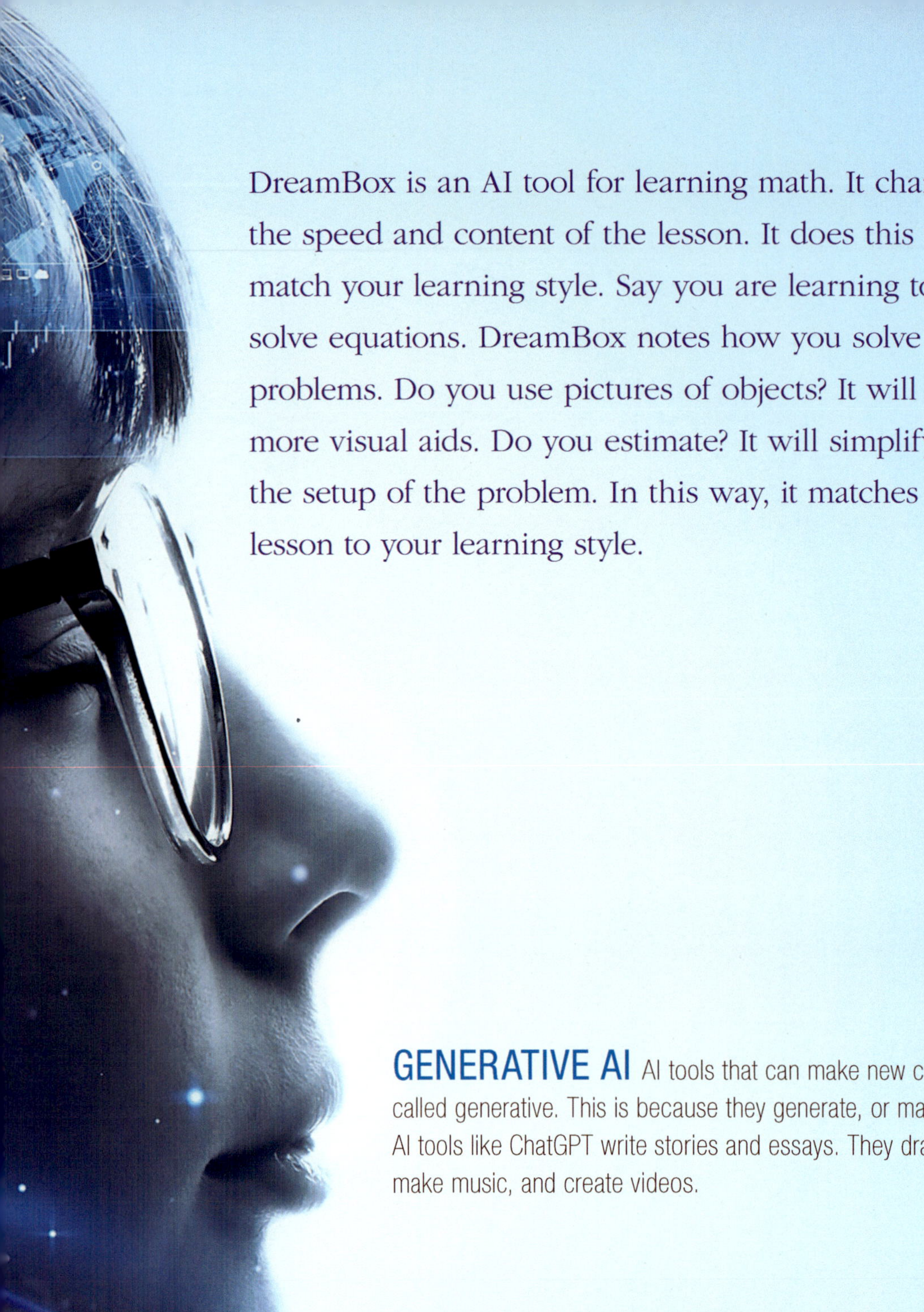

DreamBox is an AI tool for learning math. It changes the speed and content of the lesson. It does this to match your learning style. Say you are learning to solve equations. DreamBox notes how you solve problems. Do you use pictures of objects? It will give more visual aids. Do you estimate? It will simplify the setup of the problem. In this way, it matches the lesson to your learning style.

GENERATIVE AI AI tools that can make new content are called generative. This is because they generate, or make, things. AI tools like ChatGPT write stories and essays. They draw images, make music, and create videos.

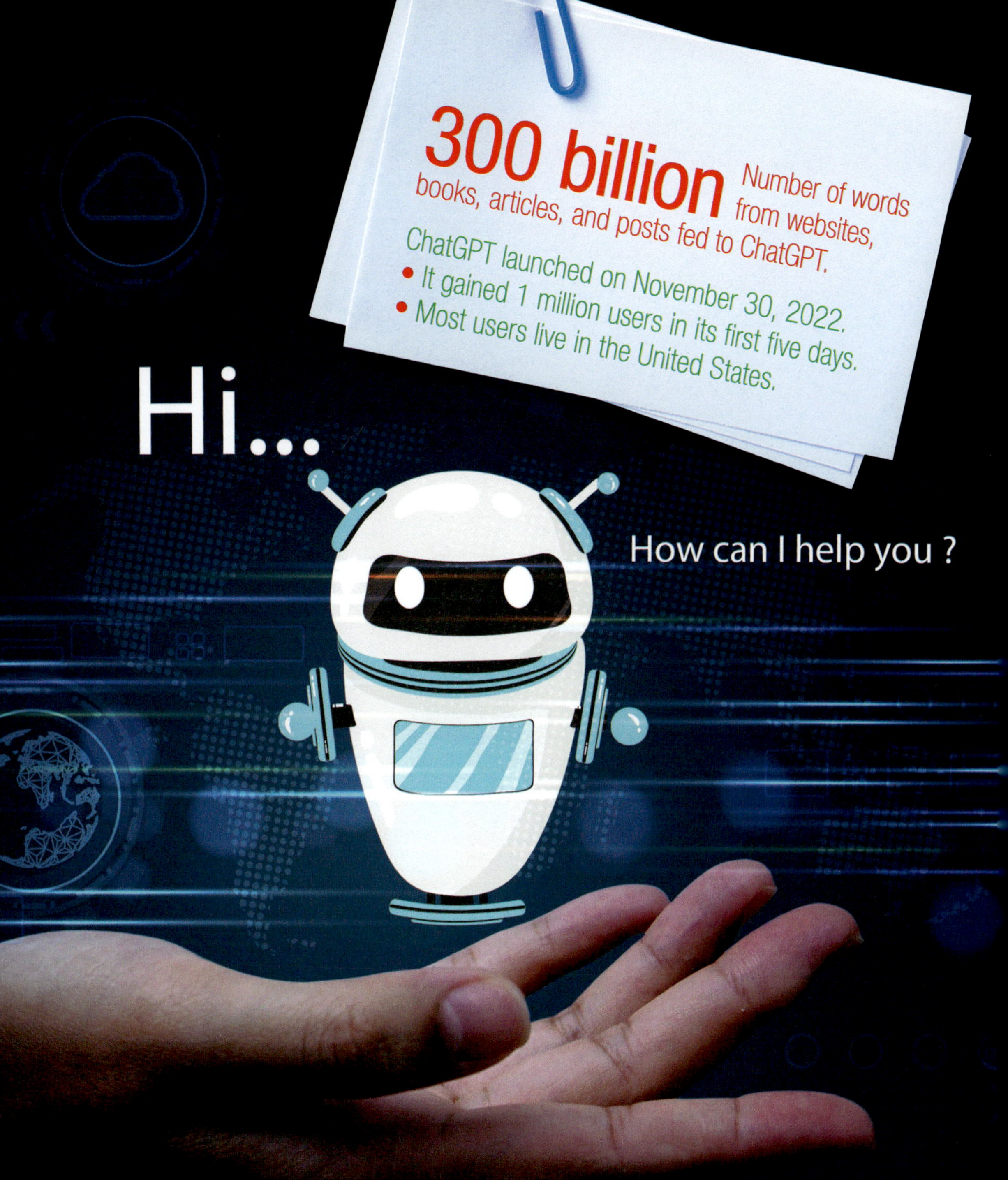

AI tools help kids explore writing, art, and even coding.

AI Helps Teachers Manage *Classrooms*

2

Teachers have a lot to do. Their main job is to help you learn. They also take attendance. They teach their students to behave well. They match their teaching style to the needs of their students. AI can help teachers by doing some of these tasks. This gives teachers more time to help you learn.

Schools need a daily count of who comes to class. AI tools such as NCheck Bio Attendance use **facial recognition**. A camera takes a picture of you as you enter class. AI can match your face to your name. It notes the date and time. It sends a report to the school office.

Teachers need to find ways to keep you on task. AI tools such as TeachFX can give them feedback to help. The app lets them record lessons with their phone or laptop. It **analyzes** the audio. It shows how long the

AI can help students learn online at home or in the classrooom.

teacher talked. It gives ideas on how teachers can ask questions, wait for answers, and respond to students. Teachers use this data to get better at teaching.

Classcraft helps teachers reward good behavior. It keeps track of how often you get work done, follow the rules, and help others.

Think About It

Some AI tools for classroom management record audio, video, and personal data of students. Do you think this is an invasion of privacy?

AI Plans Lessons *for Teachers*

3

Teachers get a curriculum from their school. It tells them what to teach. Students get computers. Teachers plan how to teach the books. AI saves teachers time by making lesson plans. They match them to the students' needs.

Education Copilot makes worksheets for teachers. A teacher can ask for five worksheets about fractions. She can ask for them to be easy, medium, and hard. She can call for problems about simplifying and comparing fractions. Copilot makes the worksheets. The teacher saves time.

Another tool is Teachaid. It helps teachers make class materials. A teacher can ask for a learning center on the solar system. Students can compare the sizes of planets. They learn what makes each planet special. They learn about orbits. Teachaid makes the materials. The teacher prints them and sets up the materials.

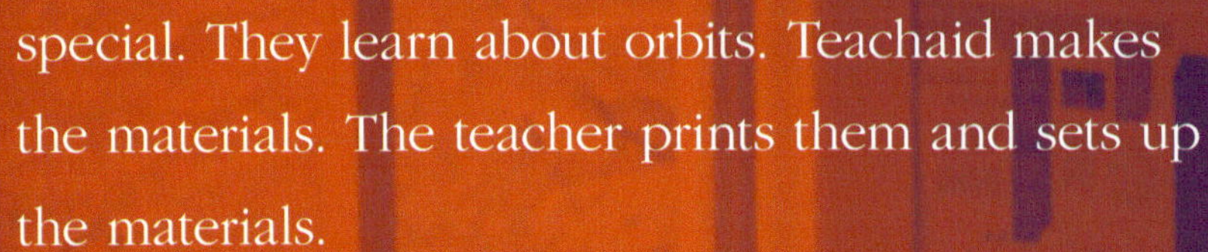

Curipod makes slide shows. Fourth graders in California study the **California Missions**. A teacher can ask for a slide show with photos of the missions. AI can also make polls and quizzes.

IT'S ALL ABOUT THE PROMPT

The phrase that you give to an AI tool is called a prompt. Learning to give the right phrase is the key to getting the best results from AI tools. "Write a lesson about seeds" will give a basic overview. "Write a lesson for third graders about the variables that affect seed growth" will give a more **targeted** response.

A teacher can plan lessons faster with AI.

4 Hours per week most elementary school teachers spend on lesson plans.

Teachers give prompts to AI tools to get better lesson plans. • These include grade level, reading level, and content needed. • AI tools save teachers time that they can spend with students.

4 AI Makes Remembering *Facts Easier*

Practice helps people learn. Sometimes you need to **memorize** facts and words. Flashcards and worksheets can help. But practice can be boring. It can turn off a student. Some teachers call this "drill and kill."

AI practice tools change things up. Quizlet makes online flashcards. You can enter your word list. It will make cards that flip to show the meaning. It makes quizzes to help you practice the words. Other tools use matching games or timed questions. The games make learning fun. Tools like this can be used for math facts, science concepts, or history lessons.

Sometimes catchy phrases help learners memorize facts. These are called **mnemonic** devices. "My Very Educated Mother Just Served Us Nachos," helps learners remember the planets in order from the sun. The first letters match

24 Percent of US teachers who reported using AI tools in 2023–24.

About 60 percent of US principals reported using AI tools for their work. • Almost 40 percent of English language arts (ELA) and science teachers used AI. • About 20 percent of US elementary and math teachers used AI.

Flashcards are a simple study tool that AI can quickly make.

the first letters of the planet names. Students can ask ChatGPT to come up with these devices.

Diffit is an online tool that helps you understand what you read. You can use it on a computer or tablet. Diffit can change the reading level to make the text easier to read. It also makes a list of new words to learn. Then it gives you questions to help you remember what you read.

AI is a good tool to create mnemonic phrases for remembering things.

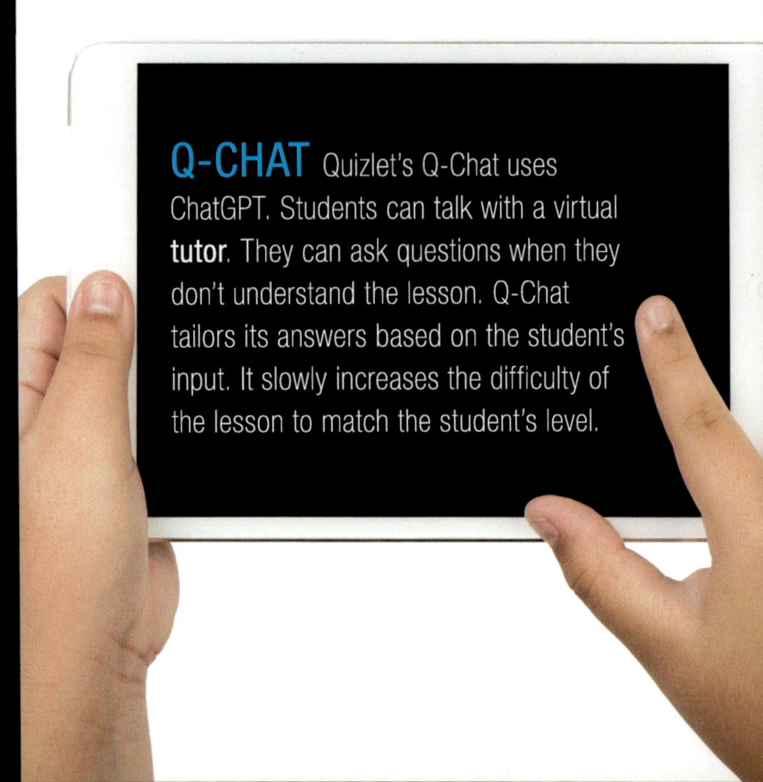

Q-CHAT Quizlet's Q-Chat uses ChatGPT. Students can talk with a virtual **tutor**. They can ask questions when they don't understand the lesson. Q-Chat tailors its answers based on the student's input. It slowly increases the difficulty of the lesson to match the student's level.

AI Helps People Learn *Languages Faster*

5

Learning a new language when you are young helps in many ways. You get better at your own language as well as the new one. You learn about grammar and sentence structure. It helps you read and write better. It improves memory and thinking skills. It's also fun to learn about new places. It might even lead to travel or a career.

Duolingo is AI for language learners. Users can speak into their device's microphone. It gives instant feedback on how to say words. It repeats the process until you are ready to move on to the next lesson. It makes worksheets and quizzes to target your needs. They are in a fun game format.

Chatbots can have what seems like real-life chats with you. You can ask and answer questions in the new language. You can pretend to be ordering at a restaurant or meeting up with friends after school.

AI can also help you learn to read and write in the new language. It changes the passage to match your level. It translates words. It checks your writing for errors and gives feedback.

Duolingo uses AI to help users learn new languages faster.

LEARNING ESL Students learning English can improve their skills with AI. Talkpal AI Chat is one such tool. It lets learners practice English any time. They can talk, listen, and write with a chatbot. Feedback is matched to the student's skill level.

Language teachers might use AI to teach Spanish.

AI Creates Real-Life Scenes to *Practice Skills*

6

You can learn a lot by pretending to be in a real-life scene. Your class might have a pretend store where you learn math. You set the price of goods. You add up sales. You count the sales tax. You make change. Your teacher might have a pretend town hall meeting. You talk about community problems and fixes. This can make learning fun and exciting. You get to make decisions and work with classmates. You learn life skills.

AI **simulations** can help students learn a wide range of topics. Virtual Zoo is like a trip to a real zoo. Kids explore the zoo online. They learn about animals. They watch them in real-time with web cams. They learn where the animals live. They learn about **ecosystems**.

AI can also teach about robotics. Rocket Launch lets kids design and launch their own rockets. This helps them learn about basic physics concepts.

Cognimates lets you make games, control robots, and develop AI models. Tensorflow playground lets you play around with neural networks. These are the computer systems that make AI tools work. They copy the way your brain works.

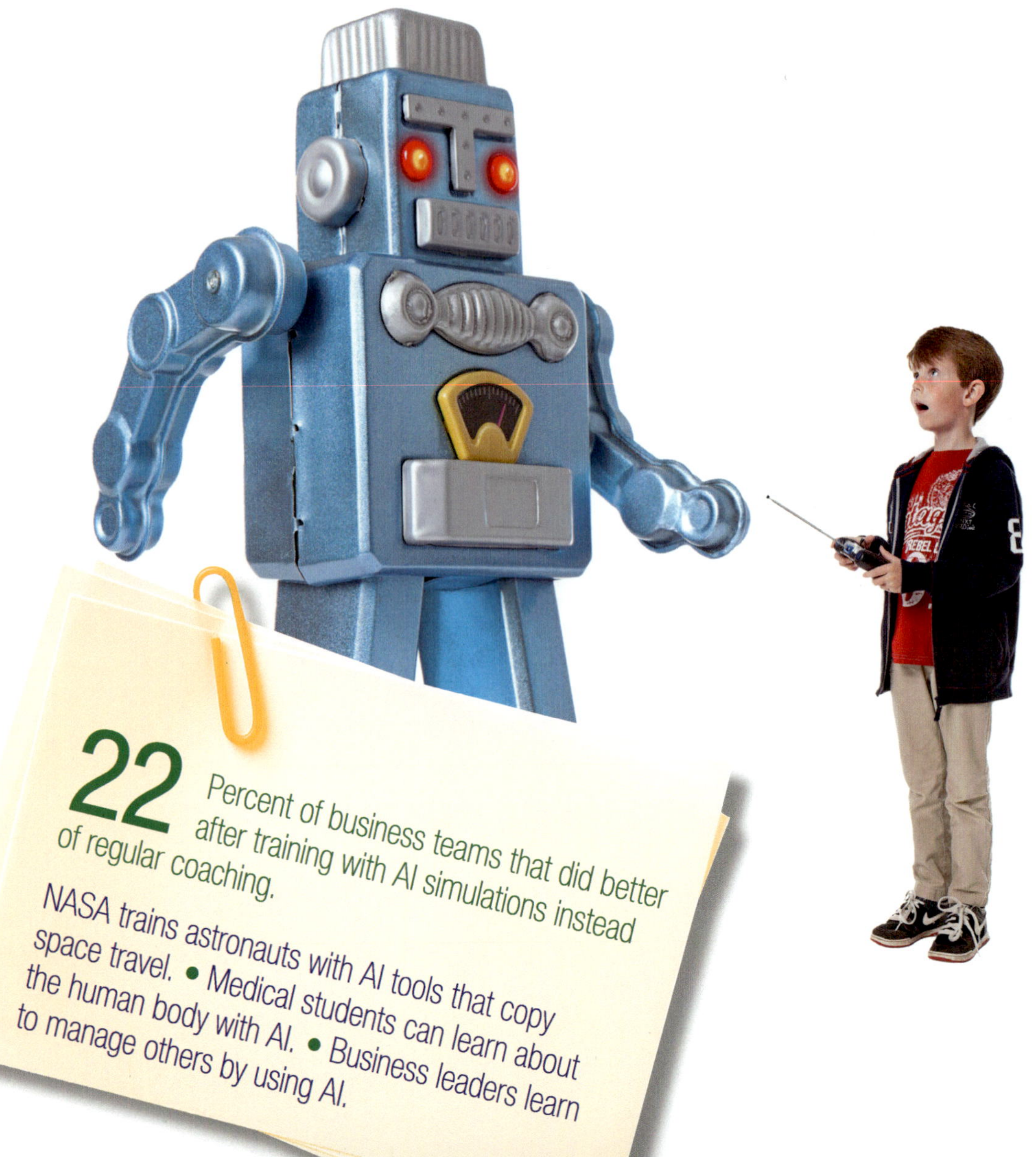

22 Percent of business teams that did better after training with AI simulations instead of regular coaching.

NASA trains astronauts with AI tools that copy space travel. • Medical students can learn about the human body with AI. • Business leaders learn to manage others by using AI.

A virtual zoo lets you explore animals from home or school.

AI Helps Students with *Disabilities*

7

AI can help students with special needs in many ways. It can change audio or speech to text. Other tools change written text to speech. AI robots help students practice social skills. These tools are useful for students who need help with seeing, reading, or communicating.

Some students cannot see well. Some cannot see at all. Other students who can see still learn better by hearing. Speechify is an AI tool that reads text aloud in a natural voice. Otter.ai is a tool that does the opposite. It works like captions on a TV show. It makes text from audio such as a teacher talking. This means students who don't hear well can still follow and learn.

Some students need extra help with social skills. They have trouble reading the looks on other people's faces. They have trouble understanding what other people are

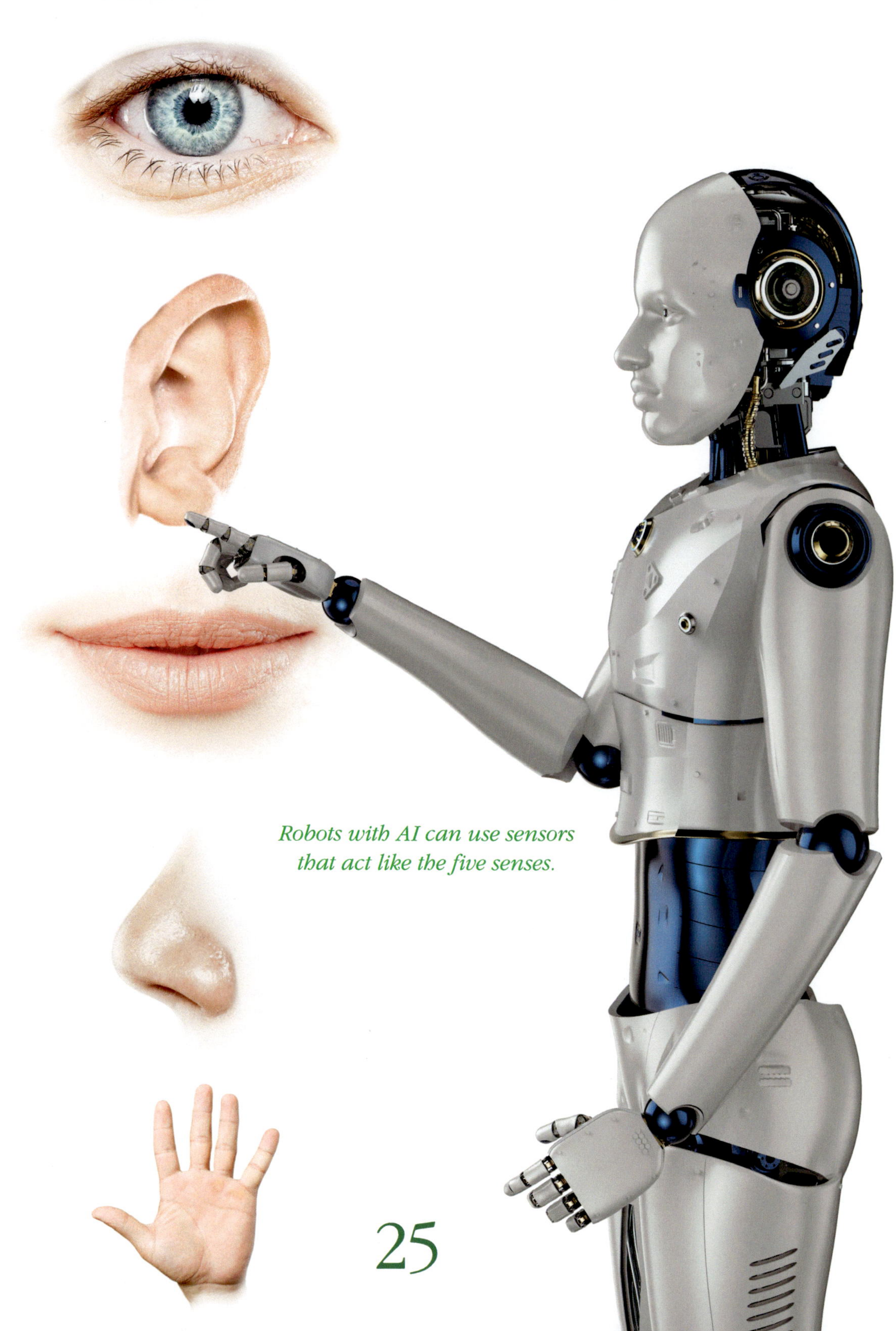

Robots with AI can use sensors that act like the five senses.

feeling. AI robots like Pepper help. The robot shows faces of people who are angry, happy, or friendly. The student can practice seeing these feelings. They practice how to act when they see them. Robots are made to be patient and comforting. This helps the student learn.

30 Minutes per day a group of children with autism used a robot to learn social skills during a one-month study at Yale.

The study took place in 2018. • The children improved at making eye contact. • They also got better at starting a conversation.

Emotion icons help kids with autism learn to recognize and name feelings.

AI Tools Can Improve *Writing Skills*

8

Writing is an important life skill. AI can help you learn to write. It can give you some ideas for topics. It helps you do research. It also gives you feedback on the structure of your writing. This helps you to improve your writing.

Suppose you need to write a report about the American Revolution. You can ask ChatGPT to give you some ideas for topics. It might suggest a key battle. It might pick a famous war leader. Once you pick a topic, you can ask for sources. Then you can go to them and learn more. As you write the report, you can ask ChatGPT to review it. ChatGPT will tell you if the structure of the report makes sense. It will give you ways to make it better.

Grammarly uses AI to find grammar and spelling errors. It will show you how to fix them. It gives the reason for the change. This helps you learn better grammar and spelling.

AI is so powerful that some people worry that students won't learn to write. They will simply get AI to write for them.

Think About It What do you think are the pros and cons of AI writing tools? Give reasons for your answer.

AI tools like Grammarly can fix grammar and spelling mistakes.

1,500 Number of teens ages 13 to 17 surveyed about their AI use in a 2024 study.
Half of the teens use AI on occasion. • Only four percent use it often. • Most common uses are finding information and brainstorming. • Students use AI to help them understand their homework.
leave

AI Creates Games to Make *Learning Fun*

9

Research shows that when you want to learn, you do better in school. When you find your lessons interesting and fun, you learn more. You get better grades. You remember more. You understand lessons better.

AI can make learning fun and appealing. Quizizz is an AI tool that helps teachers make lessons, games, and quizzes. It uses the content that the teacher gives it. Then students can compete against each other in real time. You can see your progress on a scoreboard. Quizizz has features like time limits that make the game more exciting.

Kahoot is another AI game tool. It works for reading, math, or science. Kahoot will read questions aloud for you. You can use Kahoot to learn on your own. Teachers can use Kahoot to make quizzes. They can find out what their students know.

Minecraft is a popular video game. Players build a world by using blocks to build things. Minecraft Education is an AI tool made for classrooms. By playing the game with others, you improve your communication skills. You solve problems. You work as a team. You help each other succeed. You can also learn basic coding within *Minecraft*. You make simple AI agents and program their actions and choices.

Kahoot uses AI to create quizzes and help you learn.

Minecraft Education uses AI to create fun learning adventures for students.

50 Percentage of US K–12 students who use Kahoot.

Pear Deck, Brainly, and Prodigy use AI to make learning fun. • A 2024 study found that first through eighth graders were more motivated when using technology. • Students in a 2024 study reported 54 percent of students were more engaged when using AI tools.

AI Makes Communication *in Schools Easier*

10

Communication is a big part of learning. Teachers need to stay in touch with parents. They need to talk with other teachers. Teachers and students can talk to each other in the classroom. But sometimes students have questions when they are not in school. AI makes it easier for teachers, parents, and students to talk.

Remind is an AI tool for schools. It lets your teacher send texts to you and your parents. Your teachers can remind you about homework. They can announce class events. They can send field trip information or explain an art project. They can send a message to one student, a small group, or the whole class. Remind will even translate messages into different languages. Remind keeps everyone's personal contact information private.

Teachers can also use AI to make presentations. AI can help them get ready for back-to-school night or a staff

AI makes it easier for teachers to communicate with their students.

meeting. Slidesgo is an example. Teachers can enter their speech or notes. The AI comes up with a slide show. It adds pictures. It makes a list of main points. The teacher can make changes as needed.

Think About It

Remind lets teachers and students communicate by text without revealing their phone numbers. Why do you think this is important?

AI Can Test a Student's *Progress*

11

Tests let teachers and parents know how well children are learning. The tests can show areas where students need more help. This helps teachers choose what topics need to be covered next. AI can help test students' knowledge. It can present hard topics in simpler terms so students can understand them. AI can also help teachers create, grade, and use data from tests.

Cognii is an AI tutor. It helps students practice for tests. This can help them learn and remember the content. The AI asks a question based on the content that is chosen. The student answers. Cognii then helps improve those answers.

Canvas helps teachers assess student progress. It can make lessons. It grades multiple-choice tests. It uses the results of the tests to make custom learning plans for each student.

Another tool is Conker.ai. It can make quizzes. The teacher gives it the text or the topic. They choose the type of question. It can be multiple choice, short answer, fill-in-the-blank, or true/false. They set a difficulty level. The teacher gives the number of questions they want. Conker.ai can read the questions to students. It checks the answer for the student in real time.

AI can save teachers time so they can focus more on students.

Name
Kate
A+

Colleges Use AI to *Help Students*

12

More and more colleges use AI to help pick students. Students also use AI to plan the best schedule of courses for their goals. AI can help students take notes during class. It helps them understand and remember class content.

Tens of thousands of students apply to some colleges each year. AI tools that screen students save time and money. AI can read transcripts and test scores. They study a lot of data. They choose students who are a good fit for the school. They can even scan essays and make choices. People make the final choice. But AI helps with the process.

In college, students chose a **major**. Then they need to complete a set of classes. Some classes need to be taken before others. Smart Plan uses AI to help students plan class schedules. They make sure the plan will lead to a **degree** in a set time.

Students can do better in school with the help of AI. Otter.ai, Notta, and Notes AI are tools that can give a summary of a lecture. They can take notes too. They take in speech and change it to text. They give key points. They point out main terms and concepts.

AI tools like Otter.ai take notes so students can focus on learning.

College students can use AI to better understand and remember what they learn.

80
Percentage of college admissions offices that used AI in 2024.
AI can give advisors more personal time with students who applied. • AI scheduling tools help students graduate in four years. • Students with part-time jobs fit in classes and work using AI scheduling tools.

Fact

• AI is really fast. It can read thousands of books in just a few seconds. It can use the information it learns to make predictions. It can solve problems. The more it learns, the smarter it gets.

• AI is creative. It can write stories. It can paint pictures. It can compose music. AI tools respond to user prompts. Users can keep changing their prompts until they get exactly what they want.

Sheet

• AI tools will be an important part of the future. Because they learn at such a fast speed, they will be able to solve problems that humans haven't solved.

• Some experts worry that students will use AI too much. They might not learn to do their own reading, problem-solving, and decision-making. Experts also worry that AI might not keep students' personal information safe.

Glossary

analyze
To study something closely and carefully.

California Missions
Churches built by Spanish settlers to teach Native Americans about their religion and way of life.

data
Information created or stored by a computer.

degree
A title given by a college or university.

ecosystem
A community of living things in one place.

facial recognition
A technology capable of matching a human face from a digital image or a video frame against a database of faces.

feedback
The giving back of opinions, corrections, or other comments from people who have been presented with something.

major
The main thing a student decides to study in college.

memorize
To learn completely so as to hold in the memory.

mnemonic
Assisting or attempting to assist memory.

prompt
A natural language text describing the task that an AI should perform.

simulation
Something that is made to look, feel, or behave like something real.

target
A specific goal to be achieved.

tutor
A teacher who works with students one-on-one.

For More Information

Books

Davey, Owen. *Welcome to AI: What Is Artificial Intelligence and How Will It Change Our Lives?*. London: Wide Eyed Publications, 2024.

Kaul, Jennifer. *The Potential of Artificial Intelligence.* San Diego: BrightPoint Press, 2025.

Ventura, Marne. *12 Questions about Artificial Intelligence.* Mankato, MN: Black Rabbit Books, 2025.

Websites

Artificial Intelligence (AI)
kids.britannica.com/students/article/artificial-intelligence-AI/272968

One Teacher's Take on Harnessing AI in Schools
tpt.pbslearningmedia.org/resource/one-teachers-take-on-harnessing-ai-in-school-video/pbs-newshour

Should Kids Use AI to Do Schoolwork?
www.timeforkids.com/g56/should-kids-use-ai-to-do-schoolwork-g5

About the Author

Marne Ventura is a children's book author and a former elementary school teacher. She holds a master's degree in education with an emphasis in reading and language development from the University of California.

Index

TOP RANK is published by Black Rabbit Books, P.O. Box 227, Mankato, MN, 56002. •

Edited by Ana Brauer • Designed by Danny Nanos • Photographs © Dreamstime/Dmytro Zaharchuk, 45, Polinaraulina, 32–33, ScorpionProduction, cover, 1; Getty Images/Bernhard Lang, 23, Matthias Clamer, 21, 23, powerofforever, 20, travelism, 9; Shutterstock/Asier Romero, 35, Belinda Pretorius, 48, BongkarnGraphic, 38, Casimiro PT, 37, cristovao, 36, Daniel Besic, 42–43, daniyalpro, 34, Diego Thomazini, 32, Domenico Fornas, 4, FamVeld, 15, GamePixel, 5, Gorodenkoff, 12–13, Ground Picture, 26, 40, ISARA SUKSARN, 16, Jacek Kita, 44, Jirsak, 44, jittawit21, 7, Jolygon, 46–47, Kongpraphat, 27, Kwangmoozaa, 14, 15, Lamai Prasitsuwan, 11, 28-29, lesyeuxde.er, 28, Luis Molinero, 30, 41, Maor_Winetrob, 19, 31, maxstockphoto, 8, 10, metamorworks, 6, New Africa, 2–3, 17, 18–19, 39, ozrimoz, 25, Phonlamai Photo, 2, 25, Pike-28, 16, RTimages, 22, sdx15, 41, Tom Wang, 45, Vitaly Zorkin, 37, wavebreakmedia, 24, 19 STUDIO, 31 • Printed in the United States of America.

Library of Congress Cataloging-in-Publication Data: Names: Ventura, Marne author | Title: 12 uses for artificial intelligence in education / by Marne Ventura. | Description: Mankato, MN: Top Rank, [2026] | Series: AI in the world | Includes bibliographical references and index. | Audience: Ages 9–13 | Audience: Grades 4–6 | Identifiers: LCCN 2025021452 (print) | LCCN 2025021453 (ebook) | ISBN 9781645825159 library binding | ISBN 9781645825333 paperback | ISBN 9781645825517 ebook | Subjects: LCSH: Artificial intelligence—Educational applications—Juvenile literature | Classification: LCC LB1028.43 .V46 2026 (print) | LCC LB1028.43 (ebook) | DDC 370.285/63—dc23/eng/20250510 | LC record available at https://lccn.loc.gov/2025021452